The series of *The Gold Book* is truly a blessing. *Volume 2* is on the tail of Volume 1. The goal is to make people laugh with more witty comebacks and poetic puns. I really hope you enjoy this fun filled series of The Gold Book.

"Father,

Hallowed be your name, your kingdom come. Give us each day our daily bread. Forgive us our sins, for we also forgive everyone who sins against us. And lead us not into temptation." –Luke 11:2-4

- *The Girl With The Notebook*

This man is over here thinking that I am stressing over him! Meanwhile, I am over here googling why eggs don't taste like chicken.

-Big Fine Scorpio

... and you're talking about that and I am trying to figure out why you can see the moon when it is daytime, but you can't see the sun at night.

@ The Kid

It is so cold outside,
even the bears can't
bear.

@officialtezzyjayy

PURE GOLD

Yall keep talking about how cold it is outside. Imagine how I feel being a cold ass b**** on a cold ass day.

@bell.zjanne

If I look materialistic, why would you ever approach me with no materials?

@ naeshajoanna2.0

It is an unspoken rule that if you are not pursuing God, then you do not need to be pursuing me.

@notsojaytee

GOLD.

The only EX I'm worried about is an EXample, because that's what I will make out of you.

@thereallemilli

I don't give a here
f*ck, there f*ck,
everywhere a f*ck
f*ck, old mcdonald
had a f*ck f*ck.

There is one place that I will never stop shopping at.. and that is where? De La Troi

(5 quarter store)

@shan.dawwg

GOLD!

I will separate glitter on the ground after the Pride Parade in New York City with tweezers or my tongue before I let your opinion of me stress me out. Thank you so much.

@ Leannesilvernail

Now if you're looking forward to me buying you something for Christmas, look backwards.

@Kendew94

Not all the demons have horns. Some of them have lash extensions. They walk around with racoon pu**y hairs on their eyelids.

@Pink Mango

GOLD!

The next time that a man tries to be silly with me. I am going to tell him to go back to the pond! You want to play games? Go play duck-duck goose. Go back to the pond.

I got on my slip resistant shoes so I ain't falling for nothing this year.

@dustymichael85

You are official! GOLD.

Go ahead and paint me red and black and call me *jumper cables* baby because I am about to start stuff today.

@sleevedandrelieved

Pure GOLD

I CAN TELL YOU
WHERE I AM NOT
GOING IN 2024.
ABOVE AND BEYOND,
THE EXTRA MILE OR
OUT OF MY WAY.

@Valerielovinlife

A man will have more miles than a Nissan Altima then talk about somebody for the streets. Babe, you're always touching road.

@kayl.ugh

I quit venting to
people when I realized
that vents go into
other rooms.

@nicelymade1

How are you up here ready to start a fire, but run when there is smoke?

@tallmetelly

They all know I am the big dog. Find somebody else to play with because what is firster that FIRST.

@Big Fine Scorpio

GOLD!

I aint gone lie, my motto for 2024 is "what that got to do with me?"

@hairbyskilz

I like it. I like it a lot!

When people say that they do not like me, I put on glasses to see if I give a f*ck.

@Hotmami13

You are a 3/10 on a good day and you might be a 3.5/10 if you would just shut up.

@MisterDoctorHuongyBear

Tell me I am tripping, and I know that I am not tripping so please do not fall.

@Yeahitskeith26

I am returning your nose. I found it in my business.

@snarky_nana

GOLD

Go ahead and
put a quarter in
you're a**
because you
played yourself.

@fabiansolis132

I love how you are pretending that you are not gay when I have seen less fruit at a farmers' market.

@Moonwalkonmygrave

If you can show me that you can go a whole 24/hrs without speaking to me, I will show you that I can go the whole 2024.

@ nyanogood

Gold!

Listen, her thick neck powerade pissing ass ex boyfriend....

@ iamdooney

GOLD!

Sometimes you have to sit a man down and talk to him woman to woman.

Southern Hospitality:

"we will fold your clothes with you in them if you talk to us like you ain't got no damn sense"

@ pammie_93

I am thinking of joining the cicadas this summer and screaming for 6 weeks straight.

@auntsissybeth

GOLD!

When life has you by the thong, but you just got your lashes done.

@ kewchie_mane

GOLD!

First of all; I
didn't fall for
that man! His
third leg tripped
me.

@ iamtaylorjaee

GOLD!

POETRY AT ITS FINEST!

Okay, so when standing on business... how long are we supposed to stand? Because I am ready to lay down with the business.

@ theebaldheadbaddie

POETRY AT ITS FINEST.

That is not at all what I said. You should be a DJ. You have an amazing ability to spin things.

@marcsebastianf

GOLD!

Listen, don't set yourself on fire to keep others warm.

If you go from side piece to girlfriend, you've created a job opening.

@sydneypaigebarker

GOLD

I ain't gone lie.
Bae ain't bae, if
bae don't pray!

@ notsojaytee

POETRY!

I almost lost my necklace. I forgot to take it off, it was tucked like a penis on a drag queen.

@klbowman97

GOLD

Today's lesson is:
you're my choice
not my only
option.

@ kevsoldtiktok

You expect somebody to give you the sun, the moon, and the stars and all your offering is nightlight?

@ bigbucketbishop

PURE GOLD!!

You ever thought you had a special connection with somebody just to find out you were on public WiFi?

@ just_treey

THIS IS GOLD!

Them: Hey, do you have any spare change?

Me: I don't even have a spare tire in this car!!!

@ juhkara

THIS IS GOLD!

If you ever argue with somebody and they start laughing, go ahead and hang that up like somebody yelling on your phone. That person is going to beat the grip off your shoes.

@ bigbucketbishop

Gold!

I already struggle to trust my gut. If you cannot trust a fart, you damn sure cannot trust a person.

@ iamdooney

The closest I ever want to get to science again in my life is for somebody to periodically do me on the table.

@ sun_dried_steve

Gold!

Am I the problem
or am I just the
equation that
only few can
solve?

@ dominicjjuliano

More beef in the streets than in the refrigerator.

@ hersoftlifesocial

Acknowledgements:

@ hersoftlifesocial

@ dominicjjuliano

@ sun_dried_steve

@ juhkara

@ just_treey

@ bigbucketbishop

@ kevsoldtiktok

@ notsojaytee

@sydneypaigebarker

@ambiguousmatt

@marcsebastianf

@theebaldheadbaddie

@ nyanogood

@Moonwalkonmygrave

@Fabiansolis32

@Snarky_nana

@Yeahitskeith

@MisterDoctorHuongyBear

@Hotmami13

@Big Fine Scorpio

@ Leannesilvernail

@hairbyskilz

@tallmetelly

@nicelymade1

@kayl.ugh

@Valerielovinlife

@klbowman97

@sleevedandrelieved

@dustymichael85

@certified.dululu.girl

@Pink Mango

@Kendew

@iamtaylorjaee

@kewchie_mane

@pammie_93

@dxonfairley

@iamdooney

@bell.zjanne

@billydakid2

@shan.dawwg

@savageshanez

@Unclejaytee

@TezzyJayy

I give credit on multiple pages to the names acknowledged...

THEY

DESERVE IT.

Thank you to everyone. I sincerely mean it.

Follow everyone acknowledged. I like their **quotes..**

I like it a lot!

Thank you to every single person who follows me on social media.

This is such an amazing experience and truly a blessing beyond what I could have ever imagined. God is so amazing!

Be joyful in hope,

patient in affliction,

faithful in prayer.

-Romans 12:12

Commit to the Lord whatever you do, and he will establish your plans.

- Proverbs 16:3

Thank you for The Gold Book Volume 1 and Volume 2 **and more series to come.**

Let everything that

has breath praise the

Lord.

-Psalms 150:6

CP, The Girl with

the Notebook

THIS WAS POETRY AT ITS FINEST!

-CP

Made in the USA
Columbia, SC
16 February 2025